SOMEHOW, I MANAGE

SOMEHOW, I MANAGE

The Definitive Guide to Leading Your Office and Becoming the World's Best Boss

MICHAEL G. SCOTT

TABLE OF CONTENTS

WHAT'S INSIDE

INTRODUCTION

Well you know what? My mom always used to say that average people are the most special people in the world.

And that's why God made so many.

SOMEONE HAS WRITTEN HIS OWN BOOK! HE WAS THE BEST REGIONAL MANAGER THAT THE DUNDER MIFFLIN PAPER COMPANY EVER HAD, AND NOW HE'S BACK. WHO COULD IT BE? I'LL GIVE YOU A HINT...

HE IS A MAN. A MAN YOU HAVE MISSED WITH ALL YOUR HEART. A MAN WHO HAS RUINED ALL OTHER MEN FOR YOU. WHO IS IT? WHO IS IT? WHO IS IT? IT'S MICHAEL SCOTT [WAITS FOR APPLAUSE].

I COULDN'T SLEEP LAST NIGHT. I CAME EXTRA-EARLY...SO MUCH ENERGY. [THAT'S WHAT SHE SAID] THERE ARE CERTAIN DAYS YOU KNOW YOU KNOW YOU WILL REMEMBER FOR THE REST OF YOUR LIFE, AND I JUST HAVE A FEELING THAT TODAY IS ONE OF THOSE DAYS.

I AM THE BEST BOSS. I HAVE BIG BALLS. I AM BEYONCE, ALWAYS. MY MISSION? MY MISSION IS STATED AS FOLLOWS: I WILL NOT BE BEAT. I WILL NEVER GIVE UP. I AM ON A MISSION. THAT IS THE MICHAEL SCOTT GUARANTEE.

HERE ARE SOME FUN FACTS ABOUT ME:

———————

1. I DID NOT GO TO BUSINESS SCHOOL. YOU KNOW WHO ELSE DIDN'T GO TO BUSINESS SCHOOL? LEBRON JAMES, TRACY MCGRADY, KOBE BRYANT, THEY WENT RIGHT FROM HIGH SCHOOL TO THE NBA. SO...SO THAT'S NOT THE SAME THING AT ALL.

2. MY PHILOSOPHY IS BASICALLY THIS. AND THIS IS SOMETHING THAT I LIVE BY. AND I ALWAYS HAVE. AND I ALWAYS WILL. DON'T EVER, FOR ANY REASON, DO ANYTHING TO ANYONE, FOR ANY REASON, EVER, NO MATTER WHAT...

...NO MATTER...WHERE. OR WHO, OR WHO YOU ARE WITH, OR, OR WHERE YOU ARE GOING, OR...OR WHERE YOU'VE BEEN...EVER. FOR ANY REASON, WHATSOEVER. SOMETIMES I'LL START A SENTENCE AND I DON'T EVEN KNOW WHERE IT'S GOING. I JUST HOPE I FIND IT ALONG THE WAY. LIKE AN IMPROV CONVERSATION. AN IMPROVERSATION.

3. TOY STORY, FINDING NEMO, UP. I BAWL THE ENTIRE TIME. I CAN NOT WATCH PIXAR.

———

4. I WOULD SAY MY FAVORITE ART FORM IS A TIE BETWEEN SCULPTING AND STAND-UP COMEDY.

5. MY WORST BIRTHDAY?
WHEN I WAS 7, MY MOTHER
HIRED A PONY AND A CART
TO COME TO MY HOUSE
FOR ALL THE KIDS.

———

AND I GOT A REALLY BAD
RASH FROM THE PONY.
AND ALL THE KIDS GOT TO
RIDE THE PONY AND I HAD
TO GO INSIDE. AND MY
MOTHER WAS RUBBING
CREAM ON ME FOR
PROBABLY 3 HOURS. AND I
NEVER CAME OUTSIDE. AND
BY THE TIME I GOT OUT, THE
PONY WAS ALREADY IN THE
TRUCK AND AROUND THE
CORNER.

6. I AM NOT TO BE TRUFFLED WITH.

_____

7. WHEN I RETIRE, I DON'T WANT TO BE THE GUY WHO JUST DISAPPEARS TO AN ISLAND SOMEWHERE. I WANT TO BE THE GUY WHO GIVES EVERYTHING BACK.

8. I'M NOT SUPERSTITIOUS, BUT... I'M... I AM A LITTLE-STITIOUS.

---

9. I HATE, HATE, HATE BEING LEFT OUT. WHETHER IT'S NOT BEING PICKED FOR A TEAM, OR BEING PICKED FOR A TEAM AND SHOWING UP AND REALIZING THE TEAM DOESN'T EXIST. OR THAT THE SPORT DOESN'T EXIST. I SHOULD'VE KNOWN. POOPBALL?

10. I DONT LIKE PEOPLE COMING INTO MY HOUSE AND CHANGING THINGS. I JUST WANT TO DO THINGS MY WAY.

OK, EVERYONE, AS YOU KNOW, ONE OF MY FAVORITE THINGS IS FANFARE FOR ITS OWN SAKE. SO, WITHOUT FURTHER ADO, LET'S START CLAPPING!

WHAT IS A BUSINESS?

We can't overestimate the value of computers. Yes, they are great for playing games and forwarding funny emails.

But real business is done on paper, Okay? Write that down.

WHAT IS A BUSINESS? IS IT A COLLECTION OF NUMBERS AND SALES REPORTS? SURE. BUT, IT IS MUCH MORE.

─────────

I WORKED IN A FAST FOOD RESTAURANT TO SAVE MONEY FOR SCHOOL. BUT THEN I LOST IT IN A PYRAMID SCHEME. BUT I LEARNED MORE ABOUT BUSINESS RIGHT THEN AND THERE THAN BUSINESS SCHOOL COULD EVER TEACH ME. BUSINESS IS A DOGGIE DOG WORLD. AND I AM A SHARK WHO EATS DOGGIE DOGS.

THERE ARE FOUR KINDS OF BUSINESS: TOURISM, FOOD SERVICE, RAILROADS, AND SALES. AND HOSPITALS, MANUFACTURING...AND AIR TRAVEL.

SO, YOU WANNA START A BUSINESS. HOW DO YOU START?

GOOD BUSINESS IS ABOUT RESPECT AND ACCOUNTABILITY AND FOLLOW-THROUGH. YOU DON'T JUST MAKE PROMISES AND PULL THE RUG OUT FROM UNDER SOMEBODY, DO YOU?

THE FUNDAMENTALS OF BUSINESS: "MENTAL" IS PART OF THE WORD, I HAVE UNDERLINED IT. BECAUSE YOU'RE MENTAL, IF YOU DON'T HAVE A GOOD TIME. YOU HAVE TO ENJOY IT. IN MY OPINION, BUSINESS SHOULD FEEL LIKE A NIGHT OUT.

BUSINESS IS LIKE A JUNGLE AND I AM LIKE A TIGER. THERE IS NO WAY OF KNOWING WHAT GOES ON INSIDE THE TIGER'S HEAD. WE DON'T HAVE THE TECHNOLOGY.

IN NATURE, THERE IS SOMETHING CALLED A "FOOD CHAIN." IT'S WHERE THE SHARK EATS A LITTLE SHARK. AND THE LITTLE SHARK EATS A LITTLER SHARK. AND SO ON AND SO ON. UNTIL YOU GET DOWN TO THE SINGLE-CELL SHARK. SO NOW, REPLACE SHARKS WITH PAPER COMPANIES AND THAT IS ALL YOU NEED TO KNOW ABOUT BUSINESS.

MICHAEL'S 10 RULES OF BUSINESS

I am a huge Woody Allen fan. Although I've only seen *Antz*, but, I'll tell you something. What I respect about that man, is that when he was going through all that stuff that came out in the press about how *Antz* was just a rip-off of *A Bug's Life*, he stayed true to his films.

Or at least the film that I saw, which, again, was *Antz*. The thing is...I thought *A Bug's Life* was better, much better than *Antz*.

1. YOU HAVE TO PLAY TO WIN, BUT YOU ALSO HAVE TO WIN TO PLAY

YOU CANNOT LEARN FROM BOOKS. REPLACE THESE PAGES WITH LIFE LESSONS. AND THEN...YOU WILL HAVE...A BOOK THAT IS WORTH ITS WEIGHT IN GOLD.

2. ADAPT. REACT. RE-ADAPT. APT.

PEOPLE WILL NEVER BE REPLACED BY MACHINES. IN THE END, LIFE AND BUSINESS ARE ABOUT HUMAN CONNECTIONS. AND COMPUTERS ARE ABOUT TRYING TO MURDER YOU IN A LAKE. AND TO ME THE CHOICE IS EASY.

3. DON'T LISTEN TO YOUR CRITICS, LISTEN TO YOUR FANS

SOCIETY TEACHES US THAT HAVING FEELINGS AND CRYING IS BAD AND WRONG. WELL, THAT'S BOLOGNA, BECAUSE GRIEF ISN'T WRONG. THERE'S SUCH A THING AS GOOD GRIEF. JUST ASK CHARLIE BROWN.

4. IN BUSINESS, IMAGE IS EVERYHING

-ANDRE AGASSI

A HOTEL? IT JUST GIVES OUT THIS VIBE. IT'S LIKE, OH I'M DOING BUSINESS AT THE HOTEL. IT'S KIND OF SNOOTY. HERE'S THE THING, A RESTAURANT IS THE NEW GOLF COURSE. IT'S WHERE BUSINESS GETS DONE. MY CAR IS AN INVESTMENT. RIGHT? IF I HAVE TO TAKE OUT A CLIENT OR I'M SEEN AROUND SCRANTON IN IT. I LOVE IT. I LOVE MY CAR.

5. SAFETY FIRST

I.E. DON'T BURN THE BUILDING DOWN. THAT SHOULD BE A NO-BRAINER.

───────────

IN ALL THE EXCITEMENT, I FORGOT THAT MY PRIMARY GOAL IS TO KEEP PEOPLE SAFE. WOMEN CAN'T HAVE FUN IF THEY DON'T FEEL SAFE. JAN AND I HAVE A SAFE WORD IN CASE THINGS GO TOO FAR. FOLIAGE. AND IF ONE OF US SAYS THAT WORD, THE OTHER ONE HAS TO STOP. ALTHOUGH LAST TIME, SHE PRETENDED SHE DIDN'T HEAR ME.

6. FOOL ME ONCE, STRIKE ONE. BUT FOOL ME TWICE... STRIKE THREE

HOW DO YOU UN-TELL SOMETHING? YOU CAN'T. YOU CAN'T PUT WORDS BACK IN YOUR MOUTH. WHAT YOU CAN DO IS SPREAD FALSE GOSSIP SO THAT PEOPLE THINK THAT EVERYTHING THAT'S BEEN SAID IS UNTRUE.

7. YOU MISS 100% OF THE SHOTS YOU DON'T TAKE.

-WAYNE GRETZKY

-MICHAEL SCOTT

SOMETIMES TO GET PERSPECTIVE, I LIKE TO THINK ABOUT A SPACEMAN ON A STAR, INCREDIBLY FAR AWAY. AND OUR PROBLEMS DON'T MATTER TO HIM BECAUSE WE'RE JUST A DISTANT POINT OF LIGHT. BUT HE FEELS SORRY FOR ME BECAUSE HE HAS AN INCREDIBLY POWERFUL MICROSCOPE, AND HE CAN SEE MY FACE. I'M OKAY. NO, I'M NOT.

8. INTRODUCE YOURSELF, BE POLITE.

ACTUALLY, IT'S POLITE TO ARRIVE EARLY. AND SMART. ONLY REALLY GOOD FRIENDS SHOW UP EARLY. ERGO DE FACTO: GO TO A PARTY REALLY EARLY. BECOME A REALLY GOOD FRIEND.

9. MAKE FRIENDS FIRST, MAKE SALES SECOND, MAKE LOVE THIRD...
IN NO PARTICULAR ORDER.

FRIENDS JOKE WITH ONE ANOTHER. "HEY, YOU'RE POOR." "HEY, YOUR MOMMA'S DEAD." THAT'S WHAT FRIENDS DO.

10. NEVER EVER GIVE UP.

YOU WANT TO QUIT? FOR WHAT?! BFD. NEVER EVER GIVE UP

NEVER EVER GIVE UP.

HOW TO BE THE WORLD'S BEST BOSS

People say I am the best boss. They go, "God we've never worked in a place like this before. You're hilarious" and "You get the best out of us."

I think that pretty much sums it up. Then people ask me, "Michael, how do you do it?

FIRSTLY, THE WAY I MANAGE PEOPLE IS THAT I TOUCH THEIR HEARTS AND SOULS WITH HUMOR, WITH LOVE, AND MAYBE A DASH OF RAZZLE-DAZZLE. PEOPLE EXPECT A LOT FROM MY MEETINGS. LAUGHTER. SUDDEN TWISTS. SURPRISE ENDINGS.

YOU NEED TO BE ROBIN WILLIAMS AND M. NIGHT SHYAMALAN. YOU NEED TO BE ROBIN SHYAMALAN. I AM LIKE BETTE MIDLER IN "FOR THE BOYS". GOTTA KEEP THE TROOPS ENTERTAINED.

SOMETIMES AS MANAGER, YOU HAVE TO DELIVER THE BAD NEWS. ALL I CAN DO RIGHT NOW IS PUT ON A BRAVE FACE AND BE THEIR LEADER.

———

SOME PEOPLE NEED DOZENS OF FRIENDS TO SAY "HEY HEY LOOK AT ME, I'M POPULAR" BUT NOT ME. I'M VERY PICKY. I NEED 3, MAYBE 2. WHEN YOU MEET THAT SOMEONE SPECIAL, YOU'LL JUST KNOW. BECAUSE A REAL RELATIONSHIP CAN'T BE FORCED. IT SHOULD JUST COME ABOUT EFFORTLESS...LY.

I THINK I'M A ROLE MODEL HERE. I GARNER PEOPLE'S RESPECT. I'M LIKE MR. MIYAGI AND YODA ROLLED INTO ONE.

———

WE ALL KNOW IT'S HARD TO BE A BOSS, RIGHT? YOU KNOW WHAT? LOOK AROUND YOU. THESE ARE YOUR BEST FRIENDS. THESE ARE THE PEOPLE WHO WILL OPEN THEIR HEARTS TO YOU. THEY ALL HAVE HEART-ONS FOR YOU.

I COLOR CODE ALL MY INFO. I WROTE "GAY SON" IN GREEN. GREEN MEANS GO, SO I KNOW TO GO AHEAD AND SHUT UP ABOUT IT. ORANGE MEANS "ORANGE YOU GLAD YOU DIDN'T BRING IT UP?" MOST COLORS MEAN "DON'T SAY IT."

———

HERE'S ANOTHER ONE: I MARK THINGS URGENT A, URGENT B, URGENT C, URGENT D. URGENT A IS THE MOST IMPORTANT, URGENT D YOU DON'T EVEN REALLY HAVE TO WORRY ABOUT.

I AM NOT GOING TO TELL THEM THE BAD NEWS. I DON'T SEE THE POINT OF THAT. AS A DOCTOR, YOU WOULD NOT TELL A PATIENT IF THEY HAD CANCER.

A GOOD MANAGER HAS GOT TO BE HUNGRY. HUNGRY FOR SUCCESS.

WOULD I RATHER BE FEARED OR LOVED? EASY. BOTH. I WANT PEOPLE TO BE AFRAID OF HOW MUCH THEY LOVE ME. JUST REMEMBER, YOU CAN LOVE A BOSS LIKE YOU DO A FATHER.

SOMETIMES YOU HAVE TO TAKE A BREAK FROM BEING THE KIND OF BOSS THAT'S ALWAYS TRYING TO TEACH PEOPLE THINGS. SOMETIMES YOU JUST HAVE TO BE THE BOSS OF DANCING.

I LIKE TO FIND OUT WHOSE BIRTHDAY IS COMING UP TO HAVE A LITTLE CELEBRATION FOR THEM. THERE IS NO BETTER MEDICINE THAN BIRTHDAY LUNCH. HERE'S THE THING: WHATEVER I WRITE IN THE CARD HAS TO BE REALLY, REALLY FUNNY BECAUSE PEOPLE OUT THERE ARE EXPECTING IT.

———

I'VE ALREADY SET THE BAR REALLY HIGH. AND THEY'RE ALL WORRIED ABOUT THEIR JOBS, YOU KNOW. IT'S KIND OF DARK OUT THERE. CAN YOU IMAGINE IF I WROTE SOMETHING LIKE, UH, "OH, MEREDITH. HAPPY BIRTHDAY. YOU'RE GREAT. LOVE, MICHAEL." GROSS. IF I CAN'T THROW A GOOD PARTY THEN I'M A TERRIBLE BOSS.

GAMES HAVE THE POWER TO DISTRACT PEOPLE FROM STRESSFUL SITUATIONS.

BATTLESHIP GOT ME THROUGH MY PARENTS' DIVORCE. OPERATION GOT ME THROUGH MY VASECTOMY, I.E., MY OPERATION. I DON'T THINK I WOULD HAVE BEEN ABLE TO ENDURE MY BREAKUP WITH HOLLY HAD IT NOT BEEN FOR TOSS ACROSS.

WORKING IN AN OFFICE
TAKES AN ADVANCED
SENSE OF HUMOR.

———

I LOVE MY EMPLOYEES,
EVEN THOUGH I HIT ONE OF
YOU WITH MY CAR. FOR
WHICH I TAKE FULL
RESPONSIBILITY. LOOK, I'M
JUST TRYING TO TAKE
EVERYBODY'S MIND OFF OF
THIS UNAVOIDABLE
TRAGEDY, AND ONTO MORE
POSITIVE THINGS. SO, I
THOUGHT WE SHOULD
PLANT A TREE.

WHEN IT COMES TO PAPERWORK OR QUARTERLY REPORTS, THEY ARE UNREADABLE. THEY'RE JUST NUMBERS AND BORING AND BLECH.

SO WHAT I WAS THINKING IS THAT MAYBE WE SHOULD HAVE SOME SORT OF GRAPHIC, LIKE IF WE HAVE A BAD QUARTER, PUT IN A STORM CLOUD? AND WHEN WE HAVE A GOOD QUARTER, FIREWORKS? OR A RACECAR? DOESN'T HAVE TO BE A RACECAR. USE YOUR IMAGINATION.

A BOSS IS LIKE A TEACHER. AND I AM LIKE THE COOL TEACHER. LIKE MR. HANDELL.

MR. HANDELL WOULD HANG OUT WITH US, AND HE WOULD TELL US AWESOME JOKES. AND HE ACTUALLY HOOKED UP WITH ONE OF THE STUDENTS, AND THEN, LIKE, 12 OTHER KIDS CAME FORWARD. IT WAS IN ALL THE PAPERS. REALLY RUINED EIGHTH GRADE FOR US.

BUT, BEING THE WORLD'S BEST BOSS DOES HAVE ITS DISADVANTAGES:

THERE'S ALWAYS A DISTANCE BETWEEN THE BOSS AND THE EMPLOYEES. IT IS JUST NATURE'S RULE. IT'S INTIMIDATION MOSTLY. IT'S THE AWARENESS THAT THEY ARE NOT ME. I DO THINK THAT I AM VERY APPROACHABLE AS ONE OF THE GUYS. BUT MAYBE, I JUST NEED TO BE MORE APPROACHABLE...ER.

THE PROBLEM WITH BEING A BOSS: WHEN YOU'RE TOUGH, THEY RESENT YOU. WHEN YOU'RE COOL, THEY WALK ALL OVER YOU.

I BECAME A SALESMAN BECAUSE OF PEOPLE. I LOVE MAKING FRIENDS. BUT THEN I WAS PROMOTED TO MANAGER AT A VERY YOUNG AGE AND AND I STILL TRY TO BE A FRIEND FIRST BUT WHEN YOU'RE SUCCESSFUL, YOUR COWORKERS LOOK AT YOU DIFFERENTLY.

I'M FRIENDS WITH EVERYBODY IN THIS OFFICE. BEST FRIENDS.

BUT SOMETIMES, YOUR BEST FRIENDS START COMING INTO WORK LATE. START HAVING DENTIST APPOINTMENTS THAT AREN'T DENTIST APPOINTMENTS. AND THAT IS WHEN IT'S NICE TO LET THEM KNOW THAT YOU CAN BEAT THEM UP.

THERE ARE CERTAIN THINGS THAT A BOSS DOESN'T SHARE WITH HIS EMPLOYEES:

————

1.   HIS SALARY   (THAT WOULD DEPRESS THEM)
2.   HIS BED   (THAT'S WHAT SHE SAID)
3.   _____.
4.   AND I'M NOT GOING TO TELL THEM THAT I'LL BE READING THEIR EMAILS

BUT I'LL LEAVE YOU WITH THIS...

IT'S NEVER TOO EARLY FOR ICE CREAM.

CAPTAIN THE LEADER SHIP

Let me explain something to you. I set the rules and you follow them. Blindly. Okay?

And if you have a problem with that, then you can talk to our complaint department. It's a trash can.

A GOOD MANAGER DOESN'T FIRE PEOPLE. HE HIRES PEOPLE; INSPIRES PEOPLE.

I AM THEIR LEADER AND FRIEND.

I AM MY EMPLOYEES' FEARLESS LEADER. I AM. BUT MY BOSS IS THE EVA PERRON TO MY CESAR CHAVEZ.

THIS IS NOT JUST ANOTHER PARTY, IT'S A LEADERSHIP TRAINING EXERCISE (BOOZE CRUISE ON THE LAKE IN JANUARY - IT'S CHEAPER). I AM GOING TO COMBINE ELEMENTS OF FUN, MOTIVATION, AND EDUCATION INTO A SINGLE MIND-BLOWING EVENT.

IN AN OFFICE, WHEN YOU ARE RANKING PEOPLE, MANAGER IS HIGHER THAN CAPTAIN. ON A BOAT? WHO KNOWS. IT'S NEBULOSE.

NOW ON THIS SHIP, THAT IS THE OFFICE, WHAT IS THE SALES DEPARTMENT? I SEE THE SALES DEPARTMENT AS THE FURNACE. LETS NOT GET HUNG UP ON THE FURNACE. I SEE THE SALES DEPARTMENT DOWN THERE IN THE ENGINE ROOM SHOVELING COAL INTO THE FURNACE. I MEAN...THEY WERE VERY IMPORTANT IN THE MOVIE TITANIC.

LEADER...SHIP. THE WORD SHIP IS HIDDEN INSIDE THE WORD LEADERSHIP...AS ITS DERIVATION. SO IF THIS OFFICE IS IN FACT A SHIP, AS ITS LEADER, I AM THE CAPTAIN. BUT WE'RE ALL IN THE SAME BOAT. TEAMWORK.

IT IS ABOUT PRIORITIES AND MAKING DECISIONS USING THE BOAT AS AN ANALOGY. WHAT IS IMPORTANT TO YOU? IF THE BOAT IS SINKING, WHAT DO YOU SAVE? SALESMEN AND PROFIT CENTERS!

DO I NEED TO BE LIKED?
ABSOLUTELY NOT. I LIKE TO
BE LIKED. I ENJOY BEING
LIKED. I HAVE TO BE LIKED.
BUT IT'S NOT LIKE A
COMPULSIVE NEED TO BE
LIKED. LIKE MY NEED TO BE
PRAISED.

———————

WHEN YOU HAVE
SOMEBODY'S ATTENTION,
AND THEIR EYES ARE
LIGHTING UP BECAUSE
THEY ARE VERY
INTERESTED IN WHAT YOU
HAVE TO SAY, THAT IS A
GREAT FEELING. AND I
EXPERIENCED THAT
FIRSTHAND TODAY. IT IS
WONDERFUL TO BE THE
CENTER OF ATTENTION.

HOW DO I FEEL ABOUT LOSING THE SALE? IT'S LIKE IF MICHAEL PHELPS CAME OUT OF RETIREMENT, JUMPED IN THE POOL, BELLY-FLOPPED, AND DROWNED.

———

WHAT SORT OF MOVIE WOULD RUDY HAVE BEEN IF HE HAD JUST STOPPED, GIVEN UP, AFTER TWO REJECTIONS? WOULD HAVE BEEN A LOT SHORTER. PROBABLY BEEN A LOT FUNNIER. BUT IT WOULD HAVE ULTIMATELY BEEN A DISAPPOINTMENT. I STILL WOULD HAVE SEEN IT, BUT THAT'S NOT THE POINT.

PUT THE 'CULT' IN OFFICE CULTURE

I suppose summer had to end sometime. It's sad, though, because I had a great summer. I got West Nile virus, lost a ton of weight.

Then I went back to the lake. I stepped on a piece of glass in the parking lot, which hurt. That got infected even though I peed on it. Saw 'Inception.' Or at least I dreamt I did.

THERE HAS BEEN A LOT OF TALK ABOUT NEW IDEAS TODAY. WELL, NEW IDEAS ARE FINE, BUT THEY ARE ALSO ILLEGAL BECAUSE THEY ARE A FORM OF AGEISM. WHAT? YES, I AM RIGHT.

DID YOU KNOW THAT THE AGE DISCRIMINATION AND EMPLOYMENT ACT OF 1967 PROHIBITS EMPLOYMENT DISCRIMINATION BASED ON AGE WITH RESPECT TO EMPLOYEES 40 YEARS OF AGE OR OLDER? I DID.

IN FACT, MANY CULTURES REVERE OLD PEOPLE BECAUSE OF THEIR STORYTELLING ABILITY...

...LIKE THE OLD LADY FROM TITANIC. OR THE FUNNY THINGS THAT THEY CAN DO, LIKE "WHERE'S THE BEEF?"

I AM A GOOD PERSON, AND SOMETIMES, GOOD PEOPLE DON'T GET NO RESPECT. RODNEY DANGERFIELD. I DON'T GET NO RESPECT. NO RESPECT AT ALL.

———

WHEN I WAS IN THE SANDBOX AS A KID, I GOT NO RESPECT. MY WIFE LIKES TO TALK AFTER SEX. SO SHE CALLED ME FROM A HOTEL ROOM AND SAID, "I DON'T RESPECT YOU!" AHH, THOUGHTLESS.

AW, YOU KNOW WHAT
DON'T GET NO RESPECT?
AIRPLANE FOOD. WHY
DON'T THEY JUST MAKE THE
PLANE OUT OF THE AIRLINE
FOOD? MY WIFE DON'T GET
NO RESPECT, SO...TAKE HER,
PLEASE, FOR EXAMPLE.

IF YOU DON'T GET NO
RESPECT, YOU MIGHT BE
REDNECK. RESPECT IS
NIIICE. BORAT. WHAT'S THE
DEAL WITH GRAPE-NUTS?
NO GRAPES, NO NUTS. I
DON'T GET NO RESPECT!

I JUST DON'T WANT MY EMPLOYEES THINKING THAT THEIR JOBS DEPEND ON PERFORMANCE. I MEAN, WHAT SORT OF PLACE IS THAT TO CALL HOME?

———————

SO I'M THINKING, AS A REWARD FOR OUR LOYAL CLIENTS, THAT WE CONTACT THEIR ASSISTANTS, AND WE FIND OUT WHERE THEY LIVE. AND THEN, WE GO TO THEIR HOUSES, IN THE MIDDLE OF THE SUMMER, AND GO CAROLING. IT IS A SUMMER CHRISTMAS SALE-ABRATION.

DID YOU KNOW THAT IN MOROCCO IT IS COMMON TO EXCHANGE A SMALL GIFT WHEN MEETING SOMEBODY FOR THE FIRST TIME?

IN JAPAN, YOU MUST ALWAYS COMMIT SUICIDE TO AVOID EMBARRASSMENT. IN ITALY YOU MUST ALWAYS WASH YOUR HANDS AFTER GOING TO THE BATHROOM. THIS IS CONSIDERED TO BE POLITE.

MY BOSS IS SENDING ME ABROAD TO DO A PRESENTATION TO AN INTERNATIONAL CLIENT.

AND I HAVE ALWAYS BEEN INTRIGUED BY ALL THINGS INTERNATIONAL: THE WOMEN, THE PANCAKES, THE MAN OF MYSTERY.'

EVERYONE IS GOING TO END UP DYING SOMEDAY. AND I THINK IT'S BETTER TO DIE WITH PEOPLE YOU LIKE THAN TO KNOW THAT THERE'S SOMEBODY OUT THERE THAT YOU LOVE THAT YOU'RE NOT WITH.

THE PEOPLE THAT YOU WORK WITH, ARE JUST... YOUR VERY BEST FRIENDS. THEY SAY, ON YOUR DEATHBED, YOU NEVER WISH YOU SPENT MORE TIME AT THE OFFICE. BUT I WILL. GOTTA BE A LOT BETTER THAN A DEATHBED. I ACTUALLY DON'T UNDERSTAND DEATHBEDS. I MEAN, WHO WOULD BUY THAT?

THERE IS NOTHING MORE INSULTING TO A GREAT SALESMAN THAN HAVING TO LISTEN TO A BAD SALESMAN. IT'S LIKE A GREAT BASKETBALL PLAYER HAVING TO LISTEN TO A BAD BASKETBALL PLAYER.

———————

IF THERE IS ONE THING I HATE MORE THAN THE MAFIA, IT IS A LIAR. I WISH THE MAFIA WOULD GO OUT AND KILL ALL THE LIARS. BURY THEM IN MY YARD. AND I WOULDN'T TELL THE COPS A THING. NOT THAT I WOULD BE LYING PER SE. BUT I WOULD JUST GET REALLY QUIET ALL OF A SUDDEN.

I AM TRYING TO MAKE YOUR KIDS RESPECT YOU. BECAUSE A FATHER NEEDS TO RESPECT HIS BOSS, AND KIDS DON'T RESPECT THE FATHER WHO DOESN'T RESPECT THE BOSS. DO YOU UNDERSTAND THAT LINE OF LOGIC?

WHY HAVE I STAYED AT DUNDER MIFFLIN FOR SO LONG? NOT BECAUSE OF THE PAYCHECK. 'CAUSE I COULD BE MAKING MORE MONEY AS A DOCTOR OR A PROFESSIONAL ATHLETE. I THINK IT'S BECAUSE THEY RESPECT ME. A BOSS THAT WILL NOT FIRE YOU, EVEN THOUGH YOU JUST TELL HIM OFF RIGHT TO HIS FACE OVER THE PHONE. THAT'S RESPECT.

THIS IS A PLACE OF BUSINESS. YOU ARE TO LISTEN TO OTHERS, YOU ARE TO GIVE OTHERS RESPECT, AND YOU ARE TO KEEP YOUR PERSONAL ISSUES OUT OF IT.

SOMETIMES WHAT BRINGS THE KIDS TOGETHER IS HATING THE LUNCH LADY. ALTHOUGH THAT'LL CHANGE BECAUSE BY THE END OF THE FOURTH GRADE, THE LUNCH LADY WAS THE PERSON THAT I HUNG OUT WITH THE MOST.

YOU KNOW WHAT IS THE KEY TO HAPPINESS? JOY.

SO, HAVE YOU FELT THE VIBE YET? WE WORK HARD, WE PLAY HARD. SOMETIMES WE PLAY HARD WHEN WE SHOULD BE WORKING HARD. RIGHT? I GUESS THE ATMOSPHERE THAT I'VE CREATED HERE IS THAT I'M A FRIEND FIRST, AND A BOSS SECOND, AND PROBABLY AN ENTERTAINER THIRD.

WHAT MAKES A WORK ENVIRONMENT EXCELLENT? WELL, THERE ARE MANY THINGS, I BELIEVE, THAT DO SUCH A THING OF THAT NATURE. AND ONE WOULD BE HUMOR.

———

DANCING. IT IS A PRIMAL ART FORM USED IN ANCIENT TIMES TO EXPRESS YOURSELF WITH THE BODY AND COMMUNICATE.

THIS PLACE IS NOT PRISON.
IT'S WAY BETTER THAN
PRISON.
THIS OFFICE IS THE
AMERICAN DREAM.

———————

AN OFFICE IS AS SAFE AS
THE PEOPLE IN IT. AND
SOMETIMES THOSE PEOPLE
CAN DRIVE YOU TO DO
CRAZY THINGS TO SHOW
THE DANGERS OF THE
OFFICE. THAT'S THE
DANGER I FOUND MYSELF
IN. I SAVED A LIFE. MY OWN.
AM I A HERO? I REALLY
CAN'T SAY. BUT, YES.

I PROTECT THIS OFFICE FROM THE EVIL OF DRUGS. I AM RIDICULOUSLY ANTI-DRUG. I AM SO ANTI-DRUG THAT I AM ABOVE SUSPICION IN ANY WAY THAT INVOLVES SUSPICION OR TESTING OF ANY KIND. DRUGS RUIN LIVES, PEOPLE. DRUGS DESTROY CAREERS!

TAKE CHEECH AND CHONG. EVERYONE KNOWS THAT CHEECH AND CHONG ARE FUNNY BUT JUST IMAGINE HOW FUNNY THEY'D BE IF THEY DIDN'T SMOKE POT.

LOOK TO YOUR LEFT. NOW, LOOK TO YOUR RIGHT. ONE OF THOSE PEOPLE WILL BE DEAD FROM DRUG USE AT SOME POINT IN THEIR LIVES. THIS YEAR, MORE PEOPLE WILL USE COCAINE THAN WILL READ A BOOK TO THEIR CHILDREN.

DO YOU THINK THAT SMOKING DRUGS IS COOL? DO YOU THINK THAT DOING ALCOHOL IS COOL? THE POINT IM TRYING TO MAKE WITH ALL OF THIS IS THAT I HATE DRUGS.

I LIVE BY ONE RULE: NO OFFICE ROMANCES. NO WAY. VERY MESSY. INAPPROPRIATE. NO. BUT I LIVE BY ONE OTHER RULE, "JUST DO IT" - NIKE.'

––––––––––

IF I HAD TO CHOOSE BETWEEN A ONE-NIGHT STAND AND THESE PEOPLE? I'D PICK THEM EVERY TIME. WITH THEM, IT'S AN EVERY DAY STAND AND I STILL KNOW THEIR NAMES IN THE MORNING.

THIS PLACE IS LIKE SPANIARD FLY.

NEVER, EVER, EVER SLEEP WITH YOUR BOSS. I AM SO LUCKY THAT JAN AND I ONLY GOT TO SECOND BASE.

5 STYLES OF CONFLICT RESOLUTION

A meditator's tool chest. Okay, well, before we get started, you should know that there are 5 different styles of conflict.

My Shaolin Temple-style defeats your Monkey-style!

1. LOSE/LOSE

─────────

THE FIRST STYLE IS LOSE/LOSE. IF WE DO LOSE/LOSE, NEITHER OF YOU GET WHAT YOU WANT. YOU WOULD BOTH LOSE. DO YOU WANT TO PURSUE A LOSE/LOSE NEGOTIATION?

2. LOSE/WIN

———————

NOT PRETTY.

3. WIN/LOSE

_____

COMPROMISE. NOT IDEAL.

4. WIN/WIN

OKAY, THIS IS IMPORTANT...
LET'S SEE IF WE CAN
BRAINSTORM AND FIND
SOME CREATIVE
ALTERNATIVES THAT ARE
WIN/WIN.

5. WIN/WIN/WIN

———————

THE IMPORTANT
DIFFERENCE HERE IS WITH
WIN/WIN/WIN, WE ALL WIN.
ME TOO. I WIN FOR HAVING
SUCCESSFULLY MEDIATED
A CONFLICT AT WORK!

I LOVE THIS PLACE...AND IT PAINS ME TO SEE ALL THE NEGATIVITY FESTERING. WE ARE GOING TO GET EVERYTHING OUT INTO THE OPEN WHERE IT CAN BE RESOLVED.

MOVING FORWARD

I WANT YOU TO EXPRESS
YOUR FEELINGS USING "I"
EMOTION LANGUAGE AND
NO JUDGING, OR "YOU",
STATEMENTS.

OTHER IDEAS

CAGE MATCH. CAGE MATCHES? YEAH, THEY WORK. HOW COULD THEY NOT WORK? IF THEY DIDN'T WORK, EVERYBODY WOULD STILL BE IN THE CAGE. NO ONE LEAVES UNTIL WE WORK THIS OUT.

OTHER IDEAS

YOU CAN'T OUTRUN YOUR PROBLEMS. AND THAT IS WHY THE IDEA OF A CAGE MATCH IS SO UNIVERSALLY APPEALING. BUT HERE'S THE THING ABOUT CAGE MATCHES, SOMETIMES YOU HAVE TO OPEN THE CAGE.

OTHER IDEAS

———

HUG IT OUT. THAT IS WHAT MEN SAY TO EACH OTHER AFTER A FIGHT. THEY HUG IT OUT. AND IN DOING SO, THEY LET IT GO AND WALK AWAY. AND THEY'RE DONE.

OTHER IDEAS

THE JAPANESE HAVE THIS
THING CALLED "SHIATSU
MASSAGE" WHERE THEY
DIG INTO YOUR BODY VERY
HARD AND IT IS VERY
PAINFUL AND APPARENTLY
SOME PEOPLE THROW UP.
BUT THE NEXT DAY, THEY
FEEL GREAT. I'VE NEVER
HAD ONE. THEY SOUND
AWFUL.

ONBOARDING AND "OFF" BOARDING

An intervention. It's sort of hard to describe, but really its– it's a coming together. It's a surprise party for people who are– who have addictions.

And you get in their face and you scream at them and you make them feel really badly about themselves. And then they stop.

SO, EARLIER TODAY, STANLEY SASSED ME AND TOBY GAVE ME SOME SUGGESTIONS ON HOW TO DISCIPLINE HIM. THEY DID NOT WORK, OBVIOUSLY, BECAUSE THEY WERE STUPID. SO I AM NOW GOING TO FAKE FIRE HIM...

...I'M NOT FIRING HIM. I'M NOT. JUST, WHAT I'M GOING TO DO IS, I'M GOING TO PRETEND THAT I AM FIRING HIM AND I NEED YOU TO ACT LIKE I AM FIRING HIM. DO YOU GET THAT? DO YOU GET IT? I'M TEACHING HIM A LESSON. HE NEEDS TO LEARN HUMILITY, ALRIGHT? THAT'S ALL I'M...OKAY. LET'S JUST... PLAY ACT.

YOU KNOW WHEN PEOPLE SAY GETTING FIRED WAS THE BEST THING THAT EVER HAPPENED TO THEM? I FEEL SORRY FOR THOSE PEOPLE. THAT'S THE BEST THING? REALLY? UGH.

———

THE MAIN DIFFERENCE BETWEEN ME AND DONALD TRUMP IS THAT I GET NO PLEASURE OUT OF SAYING THE WORDS, "YOU'RE FIRED". YUCK. YOU'RE FIRED. IF I HAD A CATCHPHRASE, IT'D BE "YOU'RE HIRED", AND "YOU CAN WORK HERE AS LONG AS YOU WANT"...BUT THAT'S UNREALISTIC.

THEY ALWAYS SAY THAT IT IS A MISTAKE TO HIRE YOUR FRIENDS AND THEY ARE RIGHT! SO, I HIRED MY BEST FRIENDS.

———

FOR A LOT OF THESE PEOPLE, THIS IS THE ONLY FAMILY THEY HAVE. AS FAR AS I'M CONCERNED, I'M THE WORLD'S BEST DAD.

LET'S FACE IT, MOVING TO A NEW JOB CAN BE VERY STRESSFUL. I MAKE ORIENTATION FOR NEW-COMERS BUT IT'S NOT LIKE ANY ORIENTATION ANYONE HAS EVER SEEN. IT'S FUNNY. IT'S GOT A LITTLE ZING TO IT AND I HOPE THAT IT GIVES THE FLAVOR OF WHAT WE'RE ABOUT HERE.

PEOPLE HATE PEOPLE THAT ARE DIFFERENT FROM THEM. THAT'S NATURAL. BUT YOU KNOW WHAT MAKES PEOPLE FORGET THEIR DIFFERENCES? A GREAT SHOW. THAT'S WHY I CREATED "THE INTEGRATION CELEBRATION." THIS IS THE MOMENT NEW AND OLD EMPLOYEES COME TOGETHER IN APPLAUSE.

WHAT HAPPENS TO A COMPANY IF SOMEBODY TAKES THEIR BOSS AWAY? I WILL ANSWER YOUR QUESTION WITH A QUESTION.

IT'S LIKE WHAT HAPPENS TO A CHICKEN WHEN YOU TAKE ITS HEAD AWAY. IT DIES. UNLESS YOU FIND A NEW HEAD. I NEED TO SEE WHICH ONE OF THESE PEOPLE HAVE THE SKILLS TO BE A CHICKEN HEAD.

YOU HEAR ABOUT LAYOFFS IN THE NEWS BUT WHEN YOU ACTUALLY HAVE TO DO IT YOURSELF, IT'S HEAVY STUFF. I MEAN, THESE ARE PEOPLE'S LIVES WE'RE TALKING ABOUT. I HAVE TO LET SOMEONE GO AND ITS THE HARDEST THING I'VE HAD TO DO.

HOW DO YOU FIRE SOMEONE? HOW WOULD YOU WANT TO BE TOLD SO YOU COULD STILL BE FRIENDS WITH THE PERSON FIRING YOU?
I WAIT UNTIL THE END OF THE DAY BECAUSE THE BOOK I READ SAYS WAIT UNTIL THE END OF THE DAY.

_____

ADVICE FOR THE MANAGER WITHIN

If this were Russia, yeah, sure. Everyone would go to one Santa and there would be a line around the block. And once you sat on her lap and she'd ask you what you wanted, you would say probably "freedom."

At which point the KGB would arrest you and send you to Siberia. It's a good thing Russia doesn't exist anymore.

ADVICE ON LOVE

HEY YOU GUYS, LISTEN TO ME. DON'T GET HUNG UP ON JUST ONE GIRL BECAUSE THERE ARE A WHOLE LOT OF OTHER GIRLS OUT THERE.

ANY MAN WHO SAYS HE TOTALLY UNDERSTANDS WOMEN IS A FOOL. BECAUSE THEY ARE UN-UNDERSTANDABLE. THERE'S A WISHING FOUNTAIN AT THE MALL. AND I THREW A COIN IN FOR EVERY WOMAN IN THE WORLD AND MADE A WISH.

———

I WISHED FOR JAN TO GET OVER ME. I WISHED FOR PHYLLIS, A PLASMA TV. I WISHED FOR PAM TO GAIN COURAGE. I WISHED FOR ANGELA, A HEART, AND FOR KELLY, A BRAIN.

"MICHAEL, HOW CAN YOU APPRECIATE WOMEN SO MUCH BUT ALSO DUMP ONE OF THEM?" YOU MEAN, HOW CAN I BE SO ILLOGICAL AND FLIGHTY AND UNPREDICTABLE AND EMOTIONAL?

———————

WELL, MAYBE I LEARNED SOMETHING FROM WOMEN AFTER ALL.

THEY SAY THAT YOUR WEDDING DAY GOES BY IN SUCH A FLASH THAT YOUR LUCKY IF YOU EVEN GET A PIECE OF YOUR OWN CAKE. I SAY, THAT'S CRAZY. I SAY, LET THEM EAT CAKE. MARGARET THATCHER SAID THAT ABOUT MARRIAGE. SMART BROAD.

DONT FORGET TO ASK YOURSELF SOMETHING: DO YOU EVEN LIKE HER?

AS THE IRISH POET BOBBY MCFERRIN SAYS, "DON'T WORRY, BE HAPPY."

ADVICE ON FAMILY

DO YOU THINK THEY SHOULD HAVE HAD OPEN AUDITIONS FOR THE BAND HANSON? WHAT IF NO ONE NAMED HANSON SHOWED UP? THAT WOULDN'T EVEN MAKE SENSE. OR WHAT IF THEY JUST HIRED THE LITTLEST KID AND A 50 YEAR OLD GUY WHO WAS A MURDERER? REALLY SAFE.

I WANTED YOU TO COME TO ME AND SAY, "WOW, HE IS SO GREAT." AND I WAS GOING TO SAY, "WELL, IT'S IN THE GENES." AND I WAS ACTUALLY GOING TO BE WEARING JEANS. AND I'D POINT TO THEM.

———

IT WOULD HAVE BEEN NICE TO WORK WITH MY FAMILY... THESE THINGS SELDOM WORK OUT. I DON'T KNOW HOW RINGLING BROTHERS DO IT. NIGHT AFTER NIGHT, TOWN AFTER TOWN, ALL ACROSS AMERICA. YOU WOULD THINK THEY'D BE SICK OF EACH OTHER BY NOW. BUT, CLEARLY, THEY MAKE IT WORK. AND MY HAT'S OFF TO THEM.

WE HAD A FOREIGN EXCHANGE STUDENT LIVE WITH US WHEN I WAS YOUNG. AND WE CALLED HIM MY BROTHER. AND THAT'S WHO I THOUGHT HE WAS.

UM, THEN HE WENT HOME TO WHAT IS NOW FORMERLY YUGOSLAVIA, TAKING ALL OF MY BLUE JEANS WITH HIM. AND I HAD TO SPEND THE ENTIRE WINTER IN SHORTS. THAT IS WHAT RYAN IS LIKE. A FAKE BROTHER WHO STEALS YOUR JEANS.

I WANTED TO START A COMPANY, NOT A WAR. BECAUSE IN A WAR, YOU ALWAYS FIGHT THOSE YOU ARE CLOSEST TO. AND THE GREAT TRAGEDY OF THE CIVIL WAR IS THAT BROTHER FOUGHT AGAINST BROTHER...

_____

...FOR WHAT? WHAT PURPOSE DID THAT SERVE? APART FROM ABOLISHING SLAVERY? IN THAT CASE, WAR WAS THE RIGHT CHOICE. THIS DOESN'T FEEL AS IMPORTANT THOUGH. THAT'S JUST HOW THE WORLD WORKS, I GUESS.

ADVICE ON NEGOTIATIONS

NEGOTIATIONS ARE ALL ABOUT CONTROLLING THINGS. ABOUT BEING IN THE DRIVER'S SEAT. AND MAKE ONE TINY MISTAKE, YOU'RE DEAD. I MADE ONE TINY MISTAKE. I WORE WOMEN'S CLOTHES.

CHANGE THE LOCATION OF THE MEETING AT THE LAST SECOND. TOTALLY THROWS 'EM OFF.

DECLINING TO SPEAK FIRST. MAKES THEM FEEL UNCOMFORTABLE, PUTS YOU IN CONTROL.

———

NEGOTIATION IS AN ART. BACK AND FORTH. GIVE AND TAKE. AND TODAY, BOTH DARRYL AND I TOOK SOMETHING: HIGHER SALARIES. WIN, WIN, WIN. BUT YOU KNOW, LIFE IS ABOUT MORE THAN JUST SALARIES. IT'S ABOUT PERKS.

ADVICE ON HUMOR

I LOVE INSIDE JOKES. I HOPE TO BE A PART OF ONE SOMEDAY.

I AM KING OF FORWARDS. I DON'T COME UP WITH THIS STUFF. YOU WOULDN'T JUST ARREST SOMEONE WHO IS JUST DELIVERING DRUGS FROM ONE GUY TO ANOTHER.

THERE ARE CERTAIN TOPICS THAT ARE OFF-LIMITS TO COMEDIANS: JFK, AIDS, THE HOLOCUAST. THE LINCOLN ASSISINATION JUST RECENTLY BECAME FUNNY. I NEED TO SEE THIS PLAY LIKE I NEED A HOLE IN THE HEAD. I HOPE TO LIVE IN A WORLD WHERE A PERSON COULD TELL A HILARIOUS AIDS JOKE. IT'S ONE OF MY DREAMS.

ADVICE ON ADMITTING MISTAKES

IT TAKES A BIG MAN TO
ADMIT HIS MISTAKE AND I
AM THAT BIG MAN.

HERE'S THE THING: WHEN A COMPANY SCREWS UP, BEST THING TO DO IS CALL A PRESS CONFERENCE. ALERT THE MEDIA AND THEN YOU CONTROL THE STORY. WAIT FOR THEM TO FIND OUT, AND THE STORY CONTROLS YOU. THAT'S WHAT HAPPENED TO O.J.

GUESS WHAT? I HAVE FLAWS. WHAT ARE THEY? OH, I DON'T KNOW. I SING IN THE SHOWER. SOMETIMES I SPEND TOO MUCH TIME VOLUNTEERING. OCCASIONALLY I'LL HIT SOMEBODY WITH MY CAR. SO SUE ME... NO, DON'T SUE ME. THAT IS THE OPPOSITE OF THE POINT THAT I'M TRYING TO MAKE.

NO MATTER HOW I LOOK AT THIS, I AM IN THE WRONG. AND I HAVE LOOKED AT THIS THING, LIKE A HUNDRED DIFFERENT WAYS...

...FROM MY POINT OF VIEW, FROM THEIR POINT OF VIEW, AND 98 OTHERS. AND THE BOTTOM LINE, I AM IN THE WRONG. I'M THE BAD GUY.

ADVICE ON DEATH

YESTERDAY, I WAS SCRAPING SOME GUNK OFF MY WALL SOCKETS WITH A METAL FORK AND I GAVE MYSELF THE NASTIEST SHOCK. AND WHEN I CAME TO, I HAD AN "EPIPHERY". LIFE IS PRECIOUS. AND IF I DIE, I WANT MY SON TO KNOW THE DEALIO. THE DEALIO OF LIFE.

ADVICE ON BROWN-NOSERS

THE IMPORTANT THING IS THAT I LEARED SOMETHING. I DONT WANT SOMEONE SUCKING UP TO ME BECAUSE THEY THINK I'M GOING TO HELP THEIR CAREER. I WANT THEM SUCKING UP TO ME BECAUSE THEY GENUINELY LOVE ME.

WHEN I WAS FIVE YEARS OLD I HAD THESE SPIDERMAN PAJAMAS. AND ONE NIGHT, MY MOM WAS TUCKING ME IN AND SHE TRIED TO GIVE ME A RASPBERRY ON MY TUMMY AND I TRIED TO CRAWL AWAY...

...AND WHAT HAPPENED WAS, HER EYES WERE CLOSED, AND SHE GRABBED ME. AND SHE KISSED ME ON MY BUTT. AND IT WAS JUST THE WORST. SO, I KNOW WHAT IT'S LIKE TO HAVE YOUR BUTT KISSED, LITERALLY. AND IT'S TERRIBLE.

GUM

In the streets, we didn't have any rules.

Okay, maybe one: No kicks to the groin and home for dinner.

EVERYONE LIKES THE GUY
WHO OFFERS HIM A STICK
OF GUM.

CONCLUSION

I've always wanted to be in the witness protection program. Fresh start. No debts, no baggage.

I've already got my name picked out: Lord Rupert Everton. I'm a, uh, shipping merchant who raises fancy dogs. That's the life.

CONCLUSION

I WOULD LIKE TO SAY MY GOODBYES. OKAY. GOODNIGHT, AND GOOD LUCK.

CERTIFICATE

OF EXCELLENCE

PRESENTED TO :

This achievement is a reflection of your hard work, dedication and commitment to this office. You can be proud of this accomplishment.

Michael G. Scott
Regional Manager

Dwight K. Schrute
Assistant to the Regional Manager

P: (570) 555-6453
E: Michael.Scott@DunderMifflin.com
A: Dunder Mifflin, Scranton, PA 18503

To Whom It May Concern,

The dictionary defines superlative as: Of the highest kind, quality, or order, surpassing all else, or others. Supreme. I define it as "YOU", dear reader. As a sales executive, as a leader, as a person, and as a friend, you are of the highest kind, quality, and order. Supreme.

Two forty five, behind the building. Paintball.

Regards,

Michael

MICHAEL G. SCOTT

Memo